BUY RENT SELL

100+ THINGS THAT CAN GO WRONG!

By Pamela Flynt Knight

MGF Ventures

Buy Rent Sell: 100+ Things That Can Go Wrong

CreateSpace Independent Publishing Platform
North Charleston, SC

LCCN: 2017902883
ISBN-10:1543293786
ISBN-13: 978-1543293784

FORWARD

Never were there stories of so much woe, than the stories that this book will bestow.

If I could leave my kids one thing in life, I would like to leave them my book of failures because they could learn from my mistakes. When someone can see the exact steps you took that lead to your demise they could simply just not do that. It would be a greater legacy than a book of "how to" do life. It has been said, that if all we need in life were "how to" books to be successful, we would all be successful. I venture to say most of the "how to" books have been written and can be found in your local library for free.

Pamela Knight has written a heartfelt detailed list of problems that guide you through her shortcomings and through her problems in the real estate investment game. Her easy to read style provides both knowledge and direction of what not to do when entering into real estate. Use this book of failures as your roadmap to make better decisions.

I have had the pleasure of knowing and working with Pam and I feel honored to have been asked to write the forward to her book. I have witnessed firsthand her struggles, passion, and determination. The one thing I can say with certainty about this book is she has poured her heart out on every page. To anyone entering into the world of real estate for personal or investment purposes, this book is a must read. It will help you avoid your _Rude Awakening_ because you will know _100+ Things That Can Go Wrong_.

To your success ! And may God Bless.

Humbly, James Gordon

DEDICATION

This book is dedicated to each of these who have been so valuable through this process in my life. It is also dedicated to God who brought me through the ordeal of a very bad investment, preformed a miracle in my closing and has taught me to be thankful even through the trials in life.

ACKNOWLEDGEMENTS

There are a large number of people that I need to say thank you to for all their help; friends, family, contractors, real estate agents, title company employees, and investors.

. Thank you to my sons, Stephen and Will; daughter-in-law, Amber; my brother, Bill and sister-in-law, Kay. Thank you for all the advice, encouragement and support. To my friends, small group, and former renters, thank you for your prayers. To Jodi and Regina for their help in getting this to publication, your help is appreciated.

For years of putting up with immediate needs, thanks goes to Robert Turney, Andrew Stauffer, and Lewis Dooling and their crews for all the work they did. Thank you too goes to Joe Cross for continued help and advice on the foundation and things in general and your work. You all taught me so much about repairing things.

To James Gordon and Rick & Joan Blinn a big Thank you. Without you, I would still be burdened with an ever draining investment. And to everyone at Sendera Title that worked numerous times on sales documents, thank you. Your previous work was a God send and made the final closing go quickly. And, Vanessa, it did give us some great laughs.

And to my old classmate and investor, Bob Duckworth; I appreciate all your advice and that from your agent, Brenda. Jumping into this type opportunity again might take me awhile. It's good to know someone that has been successful, that I can learn from.

TABLE OF CONTENTS

BUYING
Chapter One   The Decision   Page 9
RENTING
Chapter Two   Getting the Facts   Page 15
Chapter Three   The Applicant-The Perfect Renter   Page 19

Chapter Four   What to Know   Page 21

Chapter Five   Whose Problem Is It?   Page29
Chapter Six   Gone   Page 32

Chapter Seven   Starting Again   Page 37

SELLING
Chapter Eight   Business & Personal   Page 39

Chapter Nine   Pricing & Marketing   Page 43
Chapter Ten   The Perfect Buyer   Page 47
Chapter Eleven   Who Pays for That?   Page 51
Chapter Twelve   Financing & Closing   Page 57

Chapter Thirteen   What Elsc Is Thcre?   Page 62

BUYING

CHAPTER ONE

THE DECISION

The decision to buy or to sell is very similar. They are two sides to the same coin. This first chapter will include "buying". However, many of the subjects will be covered in later chapters dealing with "selling".

There are lots of reasons you could decide to buy, sell or rent a piece of property. Maybe you have come to the time in your life that you want something of your own; some place to raise a family. Maybe you have decided to take a chance on investing in real estate or you are already involved in it with or without a partner. If you are planning on selling you might be downsizing or upgrading. If you have an empty nest, you might want something much smaller and less work. Whatever your reasons, there are things you will want to know, especially if you are a first time homebuyer.

It has been credited to Socrates both verbatim and as a takeoff of another quote but the old saying "You don't know what you don't know" really applies to anyone tackling a new endeavor. When it comes to real estate you will want to find out what it is that you do not know. You cannot ask the right questions without knowing what to ask.

Finding out those things might mean you have to do some research. It could mean you look for advice from people you trust with a lot more experience. Remember that whoever you seek information from is going to advise you out of their experience. You can get some great information but you do not have to limit your information. There is always that odd bit of information that comes up that is so rare most people do not know about it. However, you might just need that oddity. Do not ignore what someone says because they tell you something obscure.

You do not want to allow your not knowing everything to stop you from moving forward. Our fear of the unknown robs us far too often of journeys never found because of apprehensiveness. If you know how to swim, you may want to jump in with both feet. If you do not, you will want to find someone to help you but you do not want to stay out of the water and watch others having fun. Set aside your fear and go for it. Sometimes it is necessary to learn as you follow your dreams.

If your dream is real estate, you have many avenues that can be fulfilling. They all require a degree of education and some require a license. Whatever you decide on, know what you will need to move forward. The laws change quickly in the industry so you will want to have an idea about what the law says concerning your particular field.

The peripheral careers that support real estate can be as simple as being a notary for the state where you live. There are many documents that have to be notarized and anyone closing a loan will need to be a notary. Many closing agents are going to be employees of the title company. Depending on the type of closing, you may be required to close with a title company employee who is a notary. However, there are loans that can be closed by a mobile notary and this service is used to a greater degree all the time, especially since so many closings are done outside of a title office. The notary comes to you.

It may seem that title companies are a minor part of the process of buying and selling but they play a major role. A great deal of paperwork and research must be done to make sure a piece of property can be sold. They deal with buyers, sellers, agents, attorneys, county clerks and researching. They also have to reconcile any issues that crop up.

If the title company comes across a judgment or lien in connection with the property, they must make sure that these are taken care of before the sale can go forward. These types of issues can unravel a contract. No matter which side of the sale you are on, you want to make sure you have dealt with these things or that the other person in the contract has satisfied any possible issues. Anyone who has a judgment against them cannot close without satisfying the judgment.

If you are more independent, becoming an agent or investor might be more your style. These are much riskier occupations but can be more financially rewarding. They can also be financially draining. An agent is a specialized salesman and knowing the law is vital to your work. This occupation requires a license. However, more and more successful agents are hiring administrative staff to do their paperwork. Working as an admin to an agent could help you decide if becoming an agent is something you would like to pursue. Learning all the paperwork and what is involved can give you a very realistic peak into the world of an agent.

Agents of course, must first go through training. After training they will have to pass the state test in order to acquire their license. Besides the law surrounding real estate and understanding everything within the paperwork, learning sales techniques are important. To be a really successful agent it is also helpful to understand people and to be able to read and anticipate their desires. Agents often have to deal with clients, title companies, and other agents. They may also have to deal with banks and contractors. If you are not a people person or problem solver, this is not an area you will want to explore. However, if you are good with people and willing to take the necessary risks, you might find being an agent is very rewarding.

Each listing an agent takes comes with a risk. If you do not sell the property, you do not make any money. You could have a great deal of time and energy into something that becomes null and void. If you do an open house for a client and even bake cookies and have water out for it, you could end up just being out that money. You could spend months working on something, only to have it fail. On the other hand, the sale of a house can be very rewarding. You can make money and form new relationships along the way. Your opportunities when successful in this field are wide open.

Many of the more experienced and successful agents go forward to become brokers. These are the ones that take great risks. A greater degree of education and experience is necessary to obtain this higher license. Every agent must have a broker. Technically the broker is the one "listing" the property. Brokers hire the agents and handle much of the advertising. Often it is the brokers name on the sign on a property, placing the broker's reputation at the forefront.

Of course, you might want to be an investor. Now this is a controversial step. Some will be very successful at investing in real estate. Many will not. Knowing what to look for and to do is vital to being successful. Having a great agent and title company is also important to an investor. Although you might watch some shows or speak to some investors that make it all look really easy, know that investing can be very risky. You might also want to remember that any investor offering a course to teach you the business can be making a lot of their money from selling their knowledge. Having said that, the things you can learn in the different investor courses can be invaluable. Learn from those that have been investing for awhile and have been successful at it. If you have an investor that is willing to mentor you, that is your greatest asset and blessing; especially if they do not require a financial stake to be your mentor.

If you have decided to buy, it is probably the easiest decision.   That is if you are buying for yourself.   Today's technology gives you some great advantages. You can Google what you are looking for and narrow down your choices before you ever start going house to house.

Having a real estate agent here is probably the easiest decision. Whether you are buying for yourself or as an investment, an agent can give you great advice. An agent can be a valuable asset, especially if you are just beginning to invest in properties. Even a seasoned investor appreciates a good agent by their side.

Once you have that perfect property, you can clearly see your future. If it is for yourself, your life in that house looks good. If that decision was to invest, the clarity of the decision is ...well.......good or bad, you are in it until the end. There are lots of decisions ahead.

RENTING IT

CHAPTER TWO

GETTING THE FACTS

There are a few things when you decide to rent a piece of property that you need to remember. Proceed with caution. The decisions you make at the very beginning can be like the television police detective, Monk. It can be a blessing or it can be a curse. The good thing is you get to choose the direction to take. The bad thing is that your choice does not guarantee there is going to be a blessing.

Relying on everything you have learned and your best reasoning skills does not necessarily keep you from a bad choice. There is this underlying sense that we forget about. Everyone else is not just like you. They do not expect the same things and they do not think the same way. They do not care about your property like you. So anything can go wrong.

My first piece of advice is that you seek advice. Before you can rent your property or even do any marketing you have to decide how much rent you will charge for the property. This is going to vary by neighborhood and also by availability. That will determine what you can get in rent for your property. Where rental property is in a large demand, you can get a larger monthly rental for your property. On the other hand, if the market is flooded with rent houses and apartment complexes that are doing "deals" to get people in, you are not going to be able to pull in what you might have hoped. It could take you longer than expected to find a renter. So, you might want to ask a real estate agent for their assistance.

If you are like me, you know a number of agents. Now is when you have to decide if you are going to ask a friend or look for an unfamiliar agent. The pros and cons work for either decision here. Remember that agents are in business to make money and free advice is not their objective. Whomever you choose may want to handle the rental for you or they might expect a listing when you are ready to sell.

Some you ask are more than happy to help you. They will pull some comps to assess rental prices and give you some good advice. They might even do a little analysis on why one price would be better and let you know what they expect the market to do. On the other hand some, friends or not, might just find you annoying. Their attitude might depend on their dedication to customer service. Those with a great customer service view are happy to help you and appreciate that you have come to them for counsel. They will hold out hope that you could use them to manage the rental or come to them for a later sale. You could even stroke an ego or two if you ask properly. If they do freely give you advice you will want to make note of that when you decide to hire an agent, and return to them.

BUT, there are those whose focus is strictly on making money and your interruption into their work is unappreciated. Did you not know and understand that they are a "professional" and it is a waste of their time and resources to give away free advice? If this is the person you have picked to ask, you will want to quickly choose again.

You do not have to even choose an agent whom you know. You might want to do a little research and ask someone that is a stranger but has experience in the rental field. Another option is to take a recommendation from a friend. I know a couple of investors. Some I would quickly take their advice and use whomever they recommend. However, others I would not even seek their recommendations.

Your next decision before searching for that perfect renter (perfect renter = oxymoron) is to decide on a security deposit. This is tricky. For a long time, I used my monthly rent as a guideline for the security deposit. This is probably the most common practice. Then I was given a paradigm shift when someone suggested that you never make these amounts the same because it inadvertently gives the renter the idea that the security deposit can be used as their last month's rent. Why had I not thought of that before? It is such a simple idea and exactly right. A security deposit is exactly what it says – a deposit to secure your property is not destroyed or left in disarray. It is to secure that the property is left in as good of condition as it was when the individual or family moved in. Some normal wear and tear repairs will be at your cost but others that are damage from the renter will be repaired from the deposit.

You can scratch the idea that the lease states that the security deposit IS NOT and cannot be considered part of or in whole the last month's rent. I know it is in writing. I even know that if you point it out to them that they should understand. However, there is something in the brain that tilts to "Hey, they can just use the money I already gave them!". I know the law says differently. You know the law says differently. They may even know the law says differently. Still their head goes there. So, you simply make them two different amounts and suddenly the brain confusion disappears. So do you make that more or less? Great question! Good luck with that.

Calculating the security deposit can depend on current repair costs and the area your property is in. Areas of lower income and property value can attract individuals that hold a lower view of respect for your property. In that case, you might want to raise the security amount. I would suggest a smaller amount for the security deposit where the rent is greater and the possibility of damage is smaller.

Cleaning costs can also be absorbed by the security deposit. When someone is moving into the property, you want it to be in the best possible shape. The old white glove test should not be considered irrelevant here. Some think that is an extreme measure but there are many things you want to consider. Your tenant who just moved might think they did a great job of cleaning and they might. But you want to make sure the property is in the same clean condition when they moved out as when they moved in.

Not only do the floors and walls need to be orderly and sparkling, but many more details should get attention. Dust and dirt inside cabinets should be wiped clean. The windows might need to be washed. If there is a sky light, check to see if bugs have gotten in there and died. Those would need to be cleaned out. Any appliances should be cleaned. The inside and outside of stoves and ovens need attention as well as the refrigerator. Pantry and closet floors are often ignored but should get your attention when preparing for a new renter.

If the doors have scuff marks or dings you will want to touch them up and/or clean them. That little spring stopper behind the door should be in place and unbroken. Fireplaces should be clean and you might want to have a log or two for a nicer look. Be sure and check the garage to make sure there are no major stains or cracks in the floor or walls. If there is a closet or shelves, do a quick wipe down.

By the time you finish, the entire house should shine from top to bottom. Your house will want to look its best when the next renter walks in to see it. You do not want to underestimate either the curb appeal to get them in the door, or the cleanliness factor to close the contract.

CHAPTER THREE

The Applicant - The Perfect Renter

Now that you have decided to rent and landed on prices for your rent and security deposit, it is time to find that renter. You want someone that will consider your house their home. Someone with convictions and standards that say they will care for your property as though it were their own. Time to get over that notion and look for the best you can find. Remember, perfect renter is an oxymoron.

You have more choices now. Do you use that real estate agent that was so helpful or do you put it on the market yourself? How do you put it on the market? Who is going to see it?

You are going to have many questions. And again, depending on the location of the house, you might just be able to put a sign with your phone number in the yard and that will be enough. Two things come into play. First you are going to have neighbors that have friends that want to live right in that neighborhood. Or you might be in an area that does not get much traffic and advertising is going to be highly coveted. Do not dismiss the idea of that agent entirely.

If you do this yourself, you are going to have to show the house as well as advertise the house. You are going to get emails and phone calls from a lot of people asking about the house.

Have some idea what type renter you are looking for before you throw it on the market. Even if a house is located in a nice neighborhood with a substantial rent, you are going to get calls from people asking "Is this Section 8 housing?". I know. Your first thought about Section 8 is the rundown apartment that a slumlord owns and runs. That is not necessarily the case. There are people with disabilities that get section 8 assistance. There are people trying to get back on their feet and looking for a nice place that get assistance. Then you have those people who think they can afford a property but, they need to have a reality check. Some of these poor souls just feel "entitled" to live in a place like yours. Careful! Those can be some of the worst. You can put it in the lease and they will still not care. The attitude will question why you do not understand they are "entitled" to whatever the latest thing is that they expect of you. Beware. This can be emotionally draining. They are NOT who you want in your house.

CHAPTER FOUR

What to know

There is a lot to know as a landlord. You must know the law and what your rights are as well as the renters rights. I would suggest that you either consult an attorney or find a legitimate knowledgeable, landlord organization for counsel. This is invaluable because you are going to need their help. You are going to need all types of forms. You will need a lease or rental agreement that covers both your rights and the renters. This agreement or contract will need to be appropriate for the current law in your state. You will want an application form so you can gather and evaluate your best candidates. The information on this form will need to be extensive to give you the best possible picture of the person you are considering.

Then you are going to need that move-in move-out form so you can verify the condition of the property and compare it from the time they move in and when they move out. Never shy away from taking pictures of your property. If you print them, mark the date and time. If you have the pictures digitally, you can check the "media" information which shows the date and time a picture was taken.

Eventually you will need more forms and they cover a wide range of possibilities. Do not try to go this alone. It can get you in a lot of hot water. We live in a time where it does not take much for someone to consider a lawsuit. The reasons can be many, including even the idea that you are discriminating for one reason or another. When making your decision you want to be careful to not break any discrimination laws. Knowing what forms you will need and when to use them, will help a great deal.

The forms mentioned here are just a beginning. If you decide to raise the rent or give notice to the tenant for not properly keeping up the property, there are forms. If you must evict someone, there is a form; forms for pets and many more. A good landlord agency will have these for you to access with membership. If you have an attorney, they too can advise you when you need another form.

You will also need an avenue for both credit checking and background checks. You will want to check references. All are important when it comes to making your choice as to who will occupy your property. Since you are looking for the best possible tenant, you will want as much information as possible. There are different opinions as to how to ask and evaluate applicants. Some methods are better than others. I suggest you check with several individuals who are successful to find out their approach.

You need a lease that is going to cover as much as possible. It needs to layout as many possible areas because although things often seem to be on the side of the owner, they can lean heavily to a tenant's advantage. Therefore, you want to make sure that every possible contingency is covered.

You application will have lots of information and you will want to keep it secure. Your choice of checking credit and backgrounds can be helpful. There are places available that require your applicant to enter their personal information, such as social security numbers, or drivers license numbers after you request a search. The considered tenant is notified by email and must then enter the secured website before a search is completed. Then you are notified by email with the results. This can be helpful so you are not required to keep unnecessary or private information.

Please be sure that you do not discard an application until the renter has moved on. If it becomes necessary to go to court, you may need information from the application. Also, the application should have emergency information on it that you could need.

Some of the credit/background websites might even make suggestions as to whether or not you should accept an application.

Websites that provide information services come with a cost. Unless you are willing to spend a great deal on those fees, you will want to have an application fee for each person you review. These fees are not set to make money but to cover the cost for the checks performed. This is also a way in which to weed out people who are not truly serious about renting. I have paid twenty-five or thirty dollars a person for these services.

It should all be in writing. Verbal agreements are great and if you are a kind hearted person, you are going to want informality and friendship to prevail. That is a great concept and there was a time, when a mans word was his bond, but today you want it in writing. If you are having any qualms about this issue, just watch a few days of daytime justice shows where friends are suing friends or relatives or former roommates or soul mates. You will quickly understand the need to have it in writing.

You will also want to set your attitude to separate business and personal. Keep business, business. You can make friends with your renters but decide for yourself and be sure to inform them that you draw a line between business and personal. If they cannot do that, do not become friends. Keep it on a professional level only.

If you are considering a friend or relative you might want to consider forgoing this written agreement. I would **not** advise it. These are just the type people that can be offended by your decision to keep business on a business level. They could quickly be offended by you even expecting them to put it in writing. They can question your sincerity or that you trust them. If they are unable to understand the importance of keeping things on a business level and having it in writing, they can be the ones that later take advantage of you because of your "friendship" or because you are a "relative". It could be a better idea to offend your friend or relative now and not rent to them if they are already offended by your procedures. If in doubt, watch those judges on television.

The second precaution I would give before signing a lease or rental agreement with someone is that they have time to read it. I do not like to sit down without time and feel pressured to sign something that I do not have time to even look over, much less read and evaluate. If this multi-page document is written in legalize like all contracts today, I don't like it at all. So, although it is not a normal practice by landlords, I would suggest that anyone you take an application from, be given a copy of the agreement to review. You cannot control if they read it or not but you can make sure they have the opportunity. Even if you do not approve them or sign them, you have spent a small amount on some paper and ink. You have given them the same time to evaluate the contract as you, as a landlord, take to evaluate them as a renter.

You are going to have all sorts of things people will try and get by you. Some will want Section 8 housing. Because there is usually a shortage, and if you are not set up for this avenue, they will be more than willing to sway you in that direction. I would say that if you intend to take advantage of this source, be sure to check out all the requirements and eligibility regulations before you start. Talking to a landlord that holds section 8 housing and learning the advantages and disadvantages is also a good idea.

Remember that there are many great people who find themselves in need of Section 8 assistance. This can include the disabled. So if your property is not equipped to handle the requirements you might want to dismiss the idea. The cost of upgrading something might be more than you want to undertake. At the same time, you might be able to get the property upgraded through the government because of making it accessible to someone who is handicapped.

Then there is the other end of the spectrum of people that take an attitude that they do not have to take care with your property. They might have an attitude of entitlement for their every whim or they might just not care. Either of these is bad for you. It can leave your property in shambles when vacated. That translates into a great deal of cost that might not be fully covered by a security deposit. It can also cause you a great deal of trouble during the time they occupy your property, also translating into a lot of expense. Along with the expense, it can cause a great deal of stress and aggravation. These type individuals could cause you to end up in court to receive a remedy. But again, you might receive some government assistance for these types of repairs. You will want to know what is available and what you are responsible for before taking on government assisted housing. Also know that the process of setting up for this type assistance could take some time.

You are going to have those applicants that are in dire need of help. Life has dealt them a bad hand and they need grace and mercy to move forward in life. And then you will have some that will give you a sob story because they think it will advance their cause. Be careful here. Just remember that any hand you offer to help someone up can get bitten off. You will find these same people when it comes time to collect rent. A lot of wisdom is needed to know the difference between a true need and a con. It becomes important to understand when you need to be unwavering in your conviction and a written contract and when you should show mercy. Eviction or leniency can come into question at some point. Know that there are far more giving you a sob story than those that truly need your grace and mercy. Once you extend that grace, you will need to be prepared to do it again and again. Others will most likely take advantage of your grace.

As you have already seen, there are a number of different types of renters. Every time you experience a new lease, you experience a new type of renter. Your attitude from the beginning will determine the relationship you have with them.

If you work from the beginning to be a friend and do not draw that line of distinction between friend and landlord, they can take advantage of you and most likely will. You cannot expect your renter to have your same attitude. They might not want to be your friend or you might not want to be theirs. You could be an annoyance. You might be viewed as an evil person even if you are not one. Of course, since I do not know you, you might be that hard headed, immovable, non-compassionate individual that does not want friendship from a renter. They might be your annoyance. You could be a compassionate, caring individual that embraces and loves everyone. Either way, you must find a balance in order to maintain a working relationship with your renter.

Then you have the really friendly renter. They expect you to be their friend and cannot imagine you holding a hard line on anything. They will expect leniency with repairs and rent. They can even be very compassionate and understanding with you on issues. They could have issues if you charge them a late fee because they just expected that to be waived because everyone should be so understanding.

Then you have the renter that wants out of their lease. This could be a decision they come to for a number of reasons. Usually that decision is because the lease is inconvenient to their circumstances. Let's face it. Things change. If there is anything in life you can depend on, it is change. It happens no matter how much you might make plans. Circumstances in our lives change. And those changes can bring a renter to wanting out of the lease.

These decisions might be for legitimate reasons. Maybe someone looses a job or they are transferred out of the area. Things that are out of their control happen and they must make a change. These decisions might also be "because". Because they find something else they want... or because they want to help out a friend... or because they have decided they just do not like you. It could be because you do not meet their expectations or the property is not really what they expected or their responsibilities are not what they wanted. There are a great number of reasons that a renter will want out of a lease and how you handle that can mean it is a good or bad experience.

I had a renter that decided early in their lease that I should just let them move on because well, they wanted to. Neither the property nor I was what they expected and so they wanted to make a change. The fact that I expected them to live up to the lease and thereby their word did not matter. They thought I was wrong about everything. And they did everything they could to make me break the lease. They called me about everything! The hot water heater needed to be lit. The law required a peep-hole in the door. Did I mention that the door sat next to 3 large windows making the front porch far more visible than through a peep-hole? Fortunately I kept a spreadsheet on every issue and call. It was 33 pages long by the end of 10 months. They even tried calling the city, news media and a number of agencies. In the end, they had a choice to sign an agreement to leave, or be evicted. Unfortunately they allowed their attitude to get in the way and chose eviction. They were evicted, sued me and then did not show up in court for the suit. Where they could have walked away, they ended up with a large judgment. It was inconvenient for everyone and very stressful and costly.

Remember I said you could get some hard luck stories. Well, I want to tell you about one I heard. This was a couple that truly needed some grace in their life. They did not try to hide the problems they had experienced or the trouble they were in the middle of dealing with. And that was key for me. They were dealing with the problems. They were open and honest about their circumstances, expectations for the future and their current need. I do not necessarily recommend that you offer an olive leaf to hard luck stories. However, this one, I really felt like the Lord was speaking to my heart to show compassion and to work with them.

From the beginning we set out a plan to help them move forward. And they honored me because I had shown them grace. That Christmas, this guy came over and put up my Christmas lights because he appreciated me helping them. It was certainly not because he had to. It was because he wanted to and knew it would not otherwise happen. We had a plan and they stuck to it until they were hit with yet another uncontrollable circumstance. Then we made adjustments and moved forward again. In the end, I have to admit that they left owing me some money. However, we have remained friends and when I have needed something, they would come through. I was always happy to credit their debt when they helped and every now and then would receive a payment toward that debt. We have been friends a long time now and have supported one another through some tragedies. It is a blessing of friendship and the rewards of their help that are far more valuable to me today than the money.

The out of town renter is one to be aware of accepting their application. This is a hard decision too. It is that person that is transferring from out of town and they want to sign the lease, but have not actually stepped foot on the property. This can cause both parties to face unfortunate situations. Once the lease is signed, that renter is liable even if they arrive and face something far different from their expectations. It begins a renter/landlord relationship that can be strained from the first day. That is not a circumstance you want to walk into. It is better for them to arrive and find alternative arrangements for a week and then move in. And if you are ever faced with finding an out of town place, remember that although it could be an expense for temporary living arrangements, it might be far more expensive if you move too quickly.

These and many more are the types of renters you will encounter if you rent your property for any period of time. There are good and bad, destructive, demanding and accommodating people. You have to be ready to adjust to each circumstance you face.

Know that renting is not a get rich quick opportunity. Depending on the type of renter you encounter, it could actually be very costly. This is why it is important to keep things on a business level and to know, first the law and secondly, the renter. Those three things can save you a great deal of stress as you deal with the different types of people.

CHAPTER FIVE

Whose Problem is it?

Now that you have a renter you can sit back and just collect your rent for the duration of the lease. Are you laughing yet? If you do not know how funny that statement is, you have more research to do. You should be laughing because anything can pop up. Issues can arise with the property or with the renter.

Anything that arises with the property, you have to decide if, from the lease, if it is your responsibility or that of the occupant. And depending on the issue, it could be either. Let us say the plumbing has backed up. So who calls the plumber? And who pays the plumber? These are questions that you will most likely have to consult the lease about. When the question of who has to pay is something to be decided after the problem is assessed, it is usually a good idea to call someone you know. If not, you could be stuck with a bigger than expected bill because prior arrangements were not negotiated. If the renter calls someone, pays for it and then demands payment or a reduction in rent, you will need something on your side if you have to deny it.

A receipt is needed for any and all expenses you incur. You will want this receipt, both for proof of what was done as well as tax purposes at the end of the year. If your renter cannot provide a receipt or refuses to provide one, it is okay to explain that the receipt is necessary for any reimbursement. If they are unable to provide it, they will be responsible for the cost.

I had some renters tell me once that the property was so infested when they moved in that it was unlivable and they had to call an exterminator the day they moved in at a very expensive rate. Of course, having been there earlier in the day of move-in for their walk through evaluation and having spent a lot of time in the house the prior week, I let them know their claim was not supported. Also, I need a receipt for the hundreds of dollars they said they spent before I could pay anything. I also called and got information from my exterminator I knew and the cost was very different from their demands. They never provided a receipt and I never paid their demand. Shortly thereafter, I saw the gallon of bug spray in the garage. It is funny how those denials get exposed.

There are lots of funny things that renters will call you about on your property. I had one person who was upset with me because the new dishwasher I had installed did not dry the dishes like they expected. My first thought as I listened was to ask if they understand that the big blast of moist air hitting them in the face when they opened the door was steam. What is steam? It is water in a gas form. It is wet! Ok, I did not say that but it crossed my mind. I just let them know there was nothing I could do. Although practical, the suggestion to leave the door ajar and allow some air drying was not appreciated.

There are so many things that can go wrong. Like our own bodies, the older the house, the more you can see happen. The outside is not exempt from things that can go wrong. The older a home, the older and bigger the shrubs and trees have grown. Other permanent fixtures such as fences are subject to the elements and wear and tear. Of course, the normal maintenance of watering, mowing, and trimming are the responsibility of the occupant but you can be required to take care of other things that happen outside.

Do not be surprised if you get a notice from the city about something tagged by code enforcement. This might be as simple as the yard needing to be mowed. These are often quickly solved by informing the occupant of their responsibility for an issue. However, there could be times that it requires your attention.
You could come upon an issue that time, experience or finances may limit you from dealing with immediately. You could make a decision that it is not a necessary repair. A great example is the sprinkler system. This is a great convenience but not a necessary

one. If there is a major issue, you might decide to simply dismiss the repair and let the tenant know they will have to make alternate arrangements for watering the yard. How about air conditioning and heating? These are things that can be safety issues. If it is August in Texas and the A/C goes out, this could be a necessity. However, if it is August in Hawaii, the A/C being out is not as big an issue. January in New York could require a heater immediately but January in New Mexico might allow some time to be repaired. That is when it is important to know what is in your lease and what the law says.

CHAPTER SIX

Gone

Eventually your renter is going to move out. And then you have another set of issues to face. After knowing and dealing with the renter for the duration of a lease, you will probably have a good idea how they will leave things. Even with the best renters, it is hard to expect that the property will be ready for someone to move-in immediately.

You will logically assume that you are given notice and know what day the tenant will move that you can schedule a move-out walk through. This will allow you to review the property with the tenant and the initial move-in sheet they have already signed. This allows both parties to have a good idea of any expenses that might be incurred and whose responsibility they would be. Since your tenant is expecting full return of their security deposit, you would think expected repair costs would be the norm. Surprisingly, it is not. You might want to give the tenant an idea of the repairs you immediate see that are their responsibility. They could surprise you and let you know they will take a few more hours to make those repairs themselves or to do more cleaning. That is not likely to happen. However, if it does, then you will have to decide if you are willing to accept their offer.

Do not hesitate again to take pictures of your property. Especially if you took move-in pictures. You will have evidence of their responsibility, vs. your responsibility. These pictures can show if you overlooked something that should have been done prior to move in or if you were charged for something that a prior contractor failed to accomplish but charged you for doing.

Often tenants will move-out and leave a mess to be cleaned up. This can occur for a number of reasons. They may have caused damage while living in the property and wish to not face any retribution they feel could happen. That does not stop them from expecting a full refund of the security deposit. It seems like their attitude expresses the idea that if they can ignore the problem, you should too.

If they move out and for one reason or another have acquired a negative attitude, it can greatly affect the mess they leave. The anger they feel can be reflected in the amount of damage you find. You should be prepared to find holes in walls, or broken fixtures or door frames or locks.

Anytime someone moves out, it is a good idea to change the locks. You can always save the lock from the previous lease. It is usually safe after an additional lease has passed to use the previous one. However, you might want to have three sets of locks or simply discard the previous lock. Another option is to have a locksmith out to rekey the lock and simply get new keys. It always has a cost but is one that is worth keeping your property safe.

Now is also a time that you will want to keep a careful account of your costs and if the repair is your responsibility or that of the tenants. Be sure to check the laws of your state so you know who is going to be responsible. There are a number of things that might be needed and depending on state law and how long since you have performed something; you could be hit with that cost. Some of these things are painting, extermination, cleaning or replacing the carpet, a/c filters and alarm batteries.

I think one of the most surprising expenses is light bulbs. Some people like things brighter and some like them darker. If you have a lot of bulbs, such as in multiple ceiling fans, they will often leave the sockets empty or with burnt out bulbs. Be sure and note in each room if all the bulbs are present and/or working when you do an initial move-in walk through.

If you have a renter that is basically trustworthy and clean but you have irritated them they might do something to retaliate. Their basic nature will not allow them to destroy things but they will still want to cause you problems. Trash bags and or trash could be piled all together or dirt all swept up in one place like the middle of the living room. They could leave something nasty lying around like underwear or a toilet brush. Maybe they will leave the carpet very dirty or fail to clean up after a pet has caused a stain on the carpet.

I have found that almost always, the house has to be cleaned. This includes cleaning the appliances that are in the property and cleaning the carpet. If the carpet has been so stained or worn that it cannot be cleaned, it will need to be replaced. Here is a situation where you will want to know who absorbs the responsibility for this cost. If the carpet must be replace due to normal wear and tear, it is your responsibility. If it must be cleaned or replaced because the tenant has damaged it, their security deposit can be accessed.

Although it is practical to check everything when you do a final walk through, you can miss things or forget something as small as the number of light bulbs. You too will need to check and make sure everything is in working order. Tenants do not always let you know when something goes wrong. If the ice maker goes out, they could just switch to using ice trays and keep going. There could be a burner go out on the stove or the dishwasher stop working. If it is not working, the next tenant could be calling you immediately after move in. If you determine the prior tenants were responsible and have already refunded their security deposit, you will find yourself with an unexpected expense. Your chances of holding the prior tenant responsible for those expenses are likely a pipe dream. Depending on your state law, you will have already sent an accountability of costs subtracted from the security deposit with the refund. Recanting it could be very difficult or impossible.

Although your renter will want an immediate refund, let them know the time limit the law allows and your responsibility for accountability. Use the time wisely but be sure to give your prior tenant what is due them as quickly as you can. This is probably set forth in your lease but there is always a chance they will pay no attention to it.

Whether they give you notice or whether they just leave, you still have a responsibility. The decisions you make could be dependent on the choices the renter made when they leave and it can affect their deposit, but you must determine that by the terms of the lease/rental agreement. You want to remember from the time you accept the security deposit that this is not your money to spend. It is there to cover any costs you will incur at the end of the lease that the tenants are responsible to cover. The rest is their money. My recommendation is that you set aside the security deposit in a separate savings account to avoid temptation of spending or thinking of it as your own money.

Because you will probably already have another renter and their security deposit, before you return the prior tenants funds, this account can be kept open continually.

I have a second recommendation for deposits in that same account. Because there are always repairs to be made and many at your expense, I would suggest that you set aside an amount from each months' rent to make those repairs. These funds too can be deposited into the designated savings. Just be sure to keep good records so that if you must withdraw monies from this account to do repairs, that you do not accidently dip into the tenants funds. Be sure to save this amount until they move out for necessary cleaning and repairs at that point.

Once someone has given notice, you will want to estimate your down time. There is always a period of time between tenants for you to do clean-up and repairs. If you have a great renter, this could be minimal. You might lose only a day or a weekend before you have another renter moving in. You also might lose a greater amount of time getting repairs accomplished. If sheetrock has to be repaired, there is a drying time. You cannot immediately bed, texture, paint or paper until the initial mud has dried. Depending on the weather and the drying time, this could be from a few hours up to 24 hours. Getting back to the repair could also be dependent upon the contractors availability.

You could also lose time in getting a new tenant. This availability might be lessened by being able to show the home during the time the tenant has given notice. Be sure to remember though that this time could be spent in their packing. Packing efforts can leave the house in such disarray that it is hard to get another renter. You will want the house in the best available condition when you are showing it to a new prospective renter.

The market can play an important part on your down time between renters. If people are buying more than renting, you could have a house that is empty for an extended period of time. You might want to adjust your rent expectations to avoid losing a great deal of money.

CHAPTER SEVEN

Starting Again

When your tenant has vacated the property you are ready to do it all over again. You will have to fix what is broken. Before the property is ready for the next person it has to be in order. Whether they broke things accidently, on purpose, or left a mess out of spite, you have to clean it up. Doors, windows, floors, blinds, walls, and the yard have to meet the necessary standards for your next step.

Then it's time to start all over again. By now you will have an idea of what is needed because you will have done it before or know what things were like before. You now have experience at marketing and doing those credit and background checks. You have a hint of things to look for in a prospective tenant and things to watch for to avoid problems.

That of course does not mean you are not in for any more surprises. You will always get those. Someone is going to come along with something unexpected. The surprises are as varied as the people you will encounter. Some surprises are good and others not so much. At least you now have a little understanding to move forward with what you want to do.

Maybe you have decided that going through all of this again is more than you want to handle. If you are not cut out to be a landlord you get to decide the direction you take from here. Yes, there are decisions again. You could decide to fix the place up and move in yourself. You have finally come back to the decision to do it yourself or choose a realtor. Then again, you could decide to wash your hand of it and just sell.

SELLING

CHAPTER EIGHT

Business or Personal

It does not matter if you are selling a rental property or your own home. You have decisions to make before you can sell. You want to be able to maximize your income from the sale. Since there is a wide variety of things to consider you will probably not want to go this alone. So whether you decide to use a real estate agent or sell the house yourself, you want to have someone on your side. If you decide to do this yourself, seek as much advice from people you know and do not make the mistake of thinking you know it all. Even the best, have something to learn. Even good real estate agents will seek the advise and help from others instead of trying to do things all on their own.

Some of the things you will need to consider even before you put the property on the market is the kind of financing your buyer might obtain. Each level of financing brings a different set of rules. It also can limit the number of prospective buyers you will have. You will want to think about whether or not to use an agent or sell the property yourself. Condition of the house is yet another consideration. There are a lot of considerations that go into your decision to sell.

Maybe your property is a mess and you do not have the funds to do anything with it or you do not have the patience. You might want to find an all cash buyer. With the number of investors that pop up every day, that might be easier to find than you think. Just remember they are going to have to fix things up before they "flip", rent, or move into the property. Investors are also going to expect a profit for their investment. Therefore, the price you can expect is going to be much smaller than what you might have in mind. However, a cash buyer can close quicker than other loans.

There are two types of cash buyers. You have investors that are going to expect a deep discount on the property. They will discount the current market value by approximately one third or more plus the cost for the repairs they want to make in order to re-sell or rent the property. If your repairs are extensive, you will want to do some calculations before deciding to sell to an investor. If your cost to repair, hire an agent and sell out weight the cost of time and stress, you may want to contact an investor immediately. If the repairs are not too extensive and you do not mind the time or stress, the profit you make could be an advantage for you.

The second type of cash buyer is your retail buyer. It might be hard to think that in today's economy there are people out there with enough money to buy a house without a mortgage, but they do exist. There are actually more out there than you would think. If you find a cash buyer, your closing can happen quickly. The thirty to forty-five days it takes for a contract to usually close is for the benefit of a lender and the reports and paperwork they require. The closing time can be reduced to days or only a couple of weeks with a cash buyer.

If you decide that fixing things is going to be better for you and for your pocketbook, you might want to check on pricing for needed renovations. Know up front what you want to do and what you expect to pay. You will also want to know how much value it is going to add to your property if you fix it. A good honest contractor and/or real estate agent can help here. However, you will want to consider that estimates are not actual costs. What you end up paying is most likely going to be higher than an original estimate due to unexpected conditions. Somehow, there is always something that pops up that you never expected to happen.

There are other financing options available. Each type of financing will have its own limits. If the buyer chooses a conventional loan, the pool of buyers can be larger than a cash buyer but smaller than other types of loans. At the same time, it might close a little quicker as chances of going back for repairs can be limited. Although this type loan has more lenient requirements on home repairs before a purchase, it requires the buyer to have a larger down payment. That can limit the number of available buyers.

If a buyer decides to use a VA or FHA loan, they have decided to depend on some government access. There are certain things the government will require to be fixed before they will fund the sale. You can expect some additional demands after you have negotiated a price with the seller. Depending on the repairs, and how long they take, it can extend your closing. VA and FHA loans can increase your buyer's pool, but will require greater patience and possibly time to get to your closing. It could also require additional funds from your pocket.

Government assisted loans also have different requirements as to who will pay for items at closing. Do not be surprised that closing has costs. It has a lot of costs. It will have you asking questions like "What attorney?" or "Why do I have to pay for that instead of the buyer?" If you plan up front that closing will cost you $5,000.00 to $10,000.00, if or when it costs less, you will be pleasantly surprised and have a little more in your pocket than you expected.

If you decide to hire an agent for this sale, you will also have a cost for their commission. You are looking at six percent of the sale. So, if you are selling your house for $100,000 you can figure on $6,000 of that going to the realtor for their services. This might seem a large cost but that agent does a lot for their money and if another realtor actually brings in a buyer, they have to split that cost with someone else.

You will want to find a good agent. You can be tempted to call someone you know or help, like that friend that is just getting started. All very good things and kind things to do; however, this could be an idea you could consider setting aside. Do your homework before picking an agent. Find someone that knows their business and has a good track record. You might want to talk to two or three people first. Listen to those friends who have bought or sold houses and have an idea about different agents. Do not ignore your friends, but do not decide to use them just because they are a friend. And if you are selling after having gotten advice from an agent, do not forget to consider them first. Remember, they have already done work for you for free.

If you decide to sell because of dire financial reasons, a short sale could be an option for you to consider. This involves the mortgage company and working with them. It can mean that you do not make any money on the sale but it can get you out from under a financial burden and avoid a foreclosure if you find yourself in those circumstances. A short sale may not always be practical but could be a consideration if you find yourself in this type of financial need.

The decision to sell might seem like an easy one. But once you make it, there are so many more decisions that come after. Decide wisely.

Pricing and Marketing

This is a tricky part of your whole decision. When you consider selling, there are a number of factors that can go into deciding on a price. If this is a home you have lived in for some time, your pricing might not hinge on economic factors as much as other considerations. You might just want to move to another area or a bigger or smaller home depending on the size of your family.

Upsizing for family growth is likely going to push you toward a better price for your home. Downsizing because you are older and your family is shrinking, could be a factor that gives you more time for considering the price you are offered for your property.

If you have a job transfer, relocating would be your initial consideration. Moving and time constraints could play a part in how you price your home. A quick sale could be more important to you than a better price. The company that is transferring you could place a purchase option in your consideration to sell. If it does not sell within a specific amount of time, the company would be responsible for the purchase so that neither you nor they would be inconvenienced because of a sale. You will not want to depend on such an option unless you hold a substantial position with your company.

Your home may have become a bigger burden than you are willing to maintain so you might be seeking something newer or a place with less upkeep. For older individuals, living in a retirement community or facility could be part of the consideration.

Economic factors are always a consideration when you decide to sell. Your time could be a part of those economics. The time and effort you have to put into fixing and selling could be a major consideration. If your time is more important or valuable than money, a quick sale or a smaller price could be exactly what you want. If you have the time, a bigger sale price and possibly more time is something you can factor into your sale.

The marketing of your house is always important. The way it is presented can make a big difference in how quickly you get a contract for the house. It can also mean the difference in the number of buyers that view your house and the offers you get. How it is marketed can also make a difference in the type of individuals who see the home and the prices offered.

If you are planning on selling the property yourself, you will still want to take several advertising avenues. Today there are a number of real estate websites that will advertise your property. Many buyers will put a lot of stock in what these sites say about "comps" and pricing. Some websites will even list rental trends and pricing.

You will find a lot of websites that are willing to post your information at no additional cost. It helps to boost their site and helps them with their algorithms in predicting sale and rental trends. Since so many do a lot of looking to buy from home before they get out to view houses, you want to make sure that websites are a major part of your focus. But remember, these websites cannot give you the feedback you will get from an agent. Their statistics are based solely on research and input figures. Reviewing individual details and condition of the property are not part of their evaluation.

You will probably want to consider newspaper and magazine advertising. A lot of newspapers today have ad pages that are not only on-line but in their print issues as well. You don't want to limit your options when trying to market the property.

If you are selling this by yourself, be prepared to take phone calls and to show the home. There is a lot of work involved when you do it yourself. Real Estate agents and brokers go through a lot of training for a reason.

One thing that you will be asked when people are making

their inquiries is if you will be willing to do the financing of the home yourself. I will discuss that in a later chapter.

You might want to use an agent. Different agents have different styles and experience. There are also a number of agents out there. Be sure to do a little bit of research on them before you decide to sign a sales contract with one of them.

Each one approaches all the different aspects of selling your home in a different way. One agent might not like putting signs in the yard for empty houses. They can be an invitation for vandalism, especially if you are not regularly spending time at the property. Another consideration for this approach is that sometimes, a sign in the yard is actually more advertising for an agent than for the sale of the property. If it is a high traffic, highly desirable area, it could be an advantageous consideration in your market strategy. You will want to think about these things when considering if a sign needs to be displayed to sell your property

Because they are a friend is not necessarily a reason to use them to sell your house. Because they are just getting started and you want to help them out is not a good reason either. Be sure to talk to them about their strategies. Find out how they plan on addressing marketing. You will want to know how long they have been an agent or broker. Inquire if their experience is mostly in retailing or wholesaling property. Agents who deal mostly with financial institutions and selling their properties could have a very different approach than someone who deals mostly with the public on home sales. What is their success rate for the approach you want to take? These are all questions that you will want to know before you sign up with an agent.

Recommendations from others are also a good idea. You might know someone that has bought or sold property and has good things to say about their agent or how it was marketed. Or, they might have some warnings about someone that you will want to consider not calling for help. The experience of others is important in your decision for using an agent.

Remember that any agent can and will sell your property for you. How quickly it gets done can be a major consideration in who you ask about helping. Find someone that you can work with and that you will like their approach.

Also, keep communications open. Once you are in the middle of your journey, you may find yourself disagreeing with your agent, especially if it takes more time than you expected. Do not let the difference in opinion stop you from listening to their advice. You hired them for their advice and experience. You do not want to abandon that when you are in the midst of an emotional trauma.

Emotional trauma can hit you for a number of reasons. Your decision to sell can invoke a number of emotions. You cannot allow fear or stubbornness to ambush your sale. You will want to talk through these things and be sure that you make your decisions based on sound factors and advice. Your agent can help you with that. At the same time, you can help them in the same way. If your sale continues on for some time or if you have a number of contracts that fall through, your agent may face some additional challenges and can have some feeling creep in. Remember to be an encouragement to one another.

CHAPTER TEN

The Perfect Buyer

Let me say that "The Perfect Buyer", just like "The Perfect Renter" is an oxymoron. Finding that right person can be a challenge. Considering the number of people that will have go through your house, you are going to want that perfect buyer to view it, make an offer and start moving forward to closing on the first day the house is on the market. If you are occupying the house, that becomes a real priority for you. Depending on the current market, your agent and other considerations you can figure it is going to take some time.

If it is rental property and you have a renter occupying it, there are other considerations. Speed is not always realistic. You will need to speak with the tenant and they are probably going to have to sign an agreement for realtors to show the property and when. Since realtors do not want people in the house while they are showing it, the renter may have to leave each time an appointment is set. This can be a huge inconvenience. You may also not want the tenant there. Remember the attitude of renters can be delicate. If showing the house becomes very inconvenient, they could say something to someone viewing that could destroy a sale. Or, they could have company present that thinks they are helping your renter. A statement as small as "We don't want you here." could destroy a possible sale. Remember the possible buyer does not know the person present is not the owner.

Depending on the obstacles, the time will vary. It could sell that first day or it could take months to find that right buyer. Many of the factors begin with the condition of the house. Major factors to get that quick sale include having your property in beautiful condition and correct pricing.

Depending on how your agent does marketing could depend on how they price the house on the MLS (Market Listing Service) that all agents use. They may want to price the house very close to the fair market value. They will then negotiate with buyers based on price and other factors. These negotiations are going to be a part of securing any contract regardless of how the property is priced and marketed. You will have the final say on many things in that contract. Some things will be set by law.

An agent may decide to price the property high or low. If they price it low, it could be to draw more prospective buyers and create a bidding war. It could be priced lower to sell quicker or to compensate for repairs that are needed. The pricing could be placed a little higher to get a better price or to allow for you to recover costs that you put out in the sale process.

Whether the marketing is done in a buyer's market or a seller's market will also make a difference. Availability of housing can increase or decrease the price for your property. An excessive amount of property will lower your price and is considered a buyer's market. When housing is more limited, it will increase the amount you can get when you sell and is considered a seller's market. If you try to wait for a change in the market, know that could take years. There are a lot of factors that go into how and when the market changes,

The buyers that are out looking for your home can be many or few. Depending on their circumstances, it could take you time to find that perfect buyer.

Some people are going to be looking for more home than they can actually afford. These people will probably try to acquire the property for as little as possible. However, with the number of people who are not financially savvy today, they may be trying to get around the requirements. In either case, it could slow down your closing.

Most individuals will have a pre-approval. Before looking for a house, most people will check with their bank or a mortgage advisor to find out how much they can qualify to spend on a purchase. If this step has been missed by your buyers, it can extend the amount of time for them to get approval.

If you get a cash buyer, you are going to want a "proof of funds." If they are saying they have the money it does not actually mean they have it in the bank. Make sure that you are not contracting with someone that is basing their "cash" deal on a hope of some funds they expect or they are just simply lying. Have their bank produce the proof.

Many people have already been through the financial process. They could have circumstances change before they find the property they wish to purchase. Things change so it is not unusual to be faced with the possibilities of that change happening to a buyer at any time while purchasing a house. Be prepared for anything.

You will also want to remember in your search for a buyer that you are not looking for the same type person as when you were looking for a renter. You are letting go of this property and it will be someone else's responsibility. Be sure you are emotionally ready to let go. You do not want to lose a sale because you are trying to control what happens to a house once you have sold it.

If you are selling a family home or maybe property that you have inherited after a death, you might want to find just the right person to care for it. Past memories could cloud your emotions and your willingness to let go. Do not let your grief overwhelm you if you are in such a circumstance. Let someone who is not as emotionally involved guide you through the process. An understand agent can be helpful here.

If you are using an agent, you do not know the circumstances or opinions of the buyers. If there are two agents involved, you are doubly removed from the buyer. This too can cause some people anxiety. If you are a good judge of character, you might think that you could make a better decision if you could meet the buyer or talk directly to them. Allow the agent(s) to do their job. They have your best interest at heart and may be able to negotiate something that you could never consider. Remember you are letting go.

Unless you find yourself in circumstances that will require legal help due to entanglements you have to overcome, do yourself a favor and let go of the property. Your emotions and stresses will not change the circumstances and once you are released from the property, you can find that the lessons you learned or the sweet memories are enough. Besides, the perfect buyer or perfect renter is still an oxymoron.

CHAPTER ELEVEN

Who Pays for That?

One of the things that I have learned and have said on a number of occasions is that you never buy a house without getting an inspection. Having said that, what I have learned is that there are two sides to an inspection. It can expose things that need to be fixed but it can also be pretty scary for anyone that does not understand what they are seeing in the pictures and what is being said. There is no such thing as an inspection that is perfect. So, as a seller, every time a buyer orders an inspection, my heart yells "Noooooooooo!"

Because an inspection highlights everything that is wrong with a house, I would dare say that not even a new house could get a perfect inspection. On that note, be sure if you are buying a new home, you will want to make sure the developer is reputable. Inspections are not always done for new homes. If the developer is less than honest, there are things that could leave you with unexpected expenses. For example, there was a house in an area being developed by one of these less than reputable companies. Unsuspecting individuals purchased these homes not know about an FBI investigation. Apparently there were problems with the appraisals that were being done. Also, not all the houses were finished. The lack of a completed overflow drain for an air conditioning unit caused water damage that required some major repairs because the water drained over the ceiling of one of the rooms. The paint bubbled and ruined the sheetrock. It also dumped water on the carpet.

The imperfections found by an inspector give a point for negotiation after a contract is signed. These could be minor issues to be addressed and not even worth discussing. However, there could be major changes requiring your attention prior to a close or compensations in price in order to close. Please note too that inspectors do not always note that items are "grandfathered"[1] because of the age of a house.

Banks and mortgage companies are going to want an inspection to make sure that they are not financing something that will not be a major problem for them. If the problems with the house cause a greater cost to reach the value of the appraisal, it can tank a contract.

Whoever orders and pays for an inspection report has access to it. That means that a buyer does not have to give the seller a copy of the report; and they do not always give access to the report. It can be frustrating to have a contract cancel and you don't even know why without paying out of pocket for a new report. You might be able to get a copy from the issuing company but you do not always know what company performed the inspection. Also, it can come with a price.

It is important that as a seller, if you are given the opportunity to view the inspection report, that you view it with a discerning eye. See the picture of that horrible crack in the brick. Oh! There are foundation problems that are awful! But maybe not! This could be purely a cosmetic issue. If the foundation has been repaired by a reputable company and has a good warranty that will transfer, this could be a repair the homeowner did not do. Many foundation companies do not repair the cracks in bricks and they do not do interior cracks. If you do not go back after their work is done and do the cosmetic fixes, this could cause some alarm. Old repairs that have weathered can also be alarming. Putting on a new coat of paint or doing just a little work can have everything looking good again. Anything you can show as cosmetic and that has been repaired can work in your favor.

A second issue with inspection reports is that they are measured against current standards. If you are purchasing an

---

[1] Anything "grandfathered" means that the regulations have changed but at the time of installation, this items was in code and are not subject to the current code requirements..

older home, there are many things that could be "grandfathered" because the codes have changed through the years. For instance; today GFCI plugs are required in kitchens and bathrooms. This was not always the case. But today's inspection report will show this as a defect and out of code. Inspectors are not required to know all the back codes and when they changed. Nor are they required to note they could be grandfathered due to construction age.

First time home buyers may not understand the differences between things that are cosmetic and grandfathered and the things that could be a problem. As a buyer, inspection reports can have great leverage. As a seller and someone not always allowed a copy of the report, these are things that can be challenging.

One more downside to inspection reports is that as a seller, you may not actually want to see it. If there is a larger problem you have not previously been aware of, and possibly something you need to repair, you could now be required to disclose the issue. The inspection report could be good or bad for a seller.

Appraisers are not inspectors. They will see many problems with a house and can adjust the value accordingly. Many of their calculations are based on a combination of what they see, the shape the house is in, and the value of other homes in the area. These "comps" that are done on the area is one of the reasons that your realtor can come up with a value to price your house very close to what an appraisal quotes. The more experienced the realtor, the better they will be at determining that value.

The cost of previously sold homes over the past six months to a year will play a big part in the home's value. That is why it is important that you care about the neighborhood where you reside or invest. It not only affects the value of your home, but the value of homes in the area. It is not just on your street, it can involve homes up to a one mile radius. Because your house or home has an impact on the neighborhood is the reason we have seen such a rise in Homeowner Associations in recent years.

Foreclosures in the area are also going to affect the homes appraisal. Because the cost a bank sells these properties for is usually far below the values of many other houses in the area, it can bring the price down. These lower prices deal with a couple of important factors. Foreclosed homes will often be in a much poorer shape than your average house for sale. People who have lost their home to a bank or mortgage company may try to recoup monies they have lost by removing everything not too hard to remove. This can include everything from appliances to switch plates. They could remove the ceiling fans and light fixtures. There is also a good chance that these people are going to be angry. If they have spent time and effort to work with and work out arrangements for repaying a loan with no relief, it can cause them to be angry. They can take that anger out on a home since they got nowhere with the mortgage company. That anger can result in the property being damaged both inside and out.

Their financial difficulties many not be anything of their own doing. These unexpected difficulties can lead them to try every angle for solving whatever issue has them in turmoil. On the other hand, lenders tend to stick strictly to their procedures.

The reasons for not being able to keep up with a mortgage can be vast. People can lose a job, become sick, or just simply be irresponsible. That is just a few of the root causes that can get people into trouble In the times we live in, if you do not understand that lenders do not deal on a personal level with borrowers and are only interested in their bottom line, then anger can be further aggravated. Anyone retaliating on an emotional level and not respecting an agreement or making decisions because of a moral code, can do a great deal of damage to a home.

This type of behavior is unfortunately seen far too often today. What is so surprising is that people are as quick to judge as they are to retaliate. Both attitudes of selfishness and disrespect play into the downfall of current behaviors. If a greater since of respect was demonstrated than it might help to encourage business to deal on a greater personal level instead of such a statistical level and individuals to have a greater respect for business procedures. There is still a ripple effect that can be a factor in neighborhood prices and you selling your home.

Since you will not be selling a brand new home, you can be assured that something is going to need to be fixed. Once it has been determined what needs to be fixed, you can then begin negotiations for the responsibility to fix it.

So what can go wrong? Well, that is as varied as the types of people you will deal with in buying selling or renting. You don't want to limit your thinking. If you are selling your house, you want to keep an open mind.

Three different options will come up for your consideration. First is that you will fix it before the sale is closed. Second, you might not want to deal with fixing the problem but are willing to pay for it to be done by the buyer after the sale. In that case, you could give a monetary compensation on the cost of the home. This is usually a little more than what it might actually cost to fix the problem. The added cost is your cost of convenience. The third option is that fixing the problem is one for the buyer to absorb.

When a buyer absorbs a cost for fixing a property it will most likely be for something to appeal to the buyers taste. They might want a specific type of carpet or flooring that is more costly than the seller would supply. Their taste in paint colors could be vastly different. Unfortunately, it is highly unlikely they will reveal this information during the negotiations. Therefore, one of the first two options are going to be more likely than finding something the buyer wants to put money into after the sale.

Of course there are always the unexpected last minute things that can pop up. There could be a break-in or there might be someone with the lock-box code that enters and vandalizes the property.

This can be minor or major but even if you are in the middle of a contract selling a house "as is", the buyer has the expectation of purchasing it as it was when they saw it. This means you have to take care of the damage by vandals before closing. It is a bear when that closing is just days away. If this happens it is a good idea to change the lock box code. You will also want to file a report with the police department. I realize these are very logical steps but if you have allowed your emotions to run things, you might forget some steps. In a hurry to fix things, whether for marketing or closing, the obvious can elude your thinking. You can trust me on this one. I have been there.

Chapter Twelve

Financing & Closing

    Are you the do it yourselfer? Do you feel like you need to be in control of every aspect of that house until it is completely out of your hands?   If you are considering selling your home and financing it, these might be important qualities. You will want to make several considerations.

    Your first consideration is whether or not you have a mortgage on the home and your own financial circumstances. If you are under contract with a mortgage company, chances are your contract does not allow for you to just have someone else take up the payments while you transfer the title. If you speak to many investors, this is an option they will say is a consideration for you. They will point out that as long as the payments are being made, the mortgage company just does not care. I would have to say this is most likely true. However, you are always taking a chance that the process is illegal or that the mortgage company can "call the loan".   Remember, financial institutions are focused on their balance sheet and deal with legalities. If someone with a very legalistic attitude runs across this inconsistency, it could cause you a very real problem; both financially and legally.

    This demand for payment in full or an arrest might not be what you expect. You might not think about the repercussions of breach of contract or fraud when you make the decision to owner finance something you have mortgaged. If you are not financially prepared to supply the balance on the loan, you could end up in jail and/or you and the buyer could end up in a foreclosure. For people who find this option distasteful, it is best to forego the idea. It might be too great a risk and at the very least, an immoral attitude. You need to consider the importance of having a free and clear title in order to owner finance.

    There are buyers out there that are going to make a cash

offer to you. These are people who have saved their money until they could afford to purchase a home outright. Or, it could be someone that is relocating and are able to use the equity in a previous home to pay for the one they purchase from you. If this is someone selling a home, they may want a clause in the contract for a contingency that they sell their home before closing on the one they are buying. This is not something I've seen in many years. However, this option, if you are faced with it, can place you in a position that could extend the sale of your home because of any problems they could have selling their home. I believe this option is rarely (if ever) used today but, you should know about it.

The three most used options for mortgages are Conventional, FHA and VA financing.

There are a number of things that can go wrong right in the middle of waiting on a close. You could find out in the middle of a contract that the buyer has lost a job. With many two income families today, both incomes could be part of the qualifying process when you have a couple that is purchasing the house. If one of those jobs is lost, the funding for the buyers loan could also be lost and there goes your contract. At that point, it does not matter how far you are into the contract. You will have to start all over.

You could be ready to close and in the middle of that process, but the pay-off amount the title company has requested has changed for one reason or another. Maybe the contract has taken longer than expected and the amount quoted by your mortgage company has expired. Maybe payment was processed after the payoff amount was quoted. Maybe you delayed making a payment in order to not affect the payoff and now there is a late fee added. If your contract falls through and you have to get a new contract and new payoff amount, be advised that a mortgage company might charge you for each payoff that is requested.

While looking at the payoff, there are some considerations you will want to remember. You will be responsible for a pro-rated amount on taxes and insurance. This will make a difference in the amount of equity you have in the house. The later in the year, the more you are required to pay. There is a small chance when you pay off the mortgage that you will want to request the return of the equity on your home. It may not automatically be returned. You will also want to check with the insurance company to see if you have a refund coming there as well. The mortgage company may not inform them of the sale date. So, unless you give them a call and let them know of the sale, you could forfeit monies you are due. When refunding your equity, the mortgage company may access some costs. They will want to recover the filing fee for your release of lien and they could charge you for each payoff amount that is requested.

You may simply have someone back out of the sale. An inspectors report can change the buyers decision. This can happen for a number of reasons. There may be too many repairs needed for the buyer to accept; or, you might not be able to settle on what will and will not be repaired prior to a sale.

Your buyer might realize after an inspection, that what they really need is property that has less upkeep. Their circumstances might be due to the loss of a spouse and an increase in their responsibilities beyond what they thought they could manage. Age could play a part. Either an older person who has come to a place where they are physically unable to do all the things they have done or it could be they are too young and inexperienced to realize the magnitude of their responsibilities.

If you have involved someone else along the way in your ownership it could play a part. When you decide to sell, the other party could rightfully or incorrectly step in to claim what they believe is their part of profits. This can come in the form of many different ways.

Someone could place a lien on the property. If you failed to pay someone for their services, they might have placed a lien on the property. Before the house can be sold, this lien would have to be satisfied. You might be able to work with the title company to pay what is due at closing on a lien.

You could have a private arrangement with someone who believes they are owed. The sale could be stopped through a legal process. You could find yourself in the middle of a lawsuit. Proof of monies spent or agreements made over many years might have to be provided in order to settle things. If this happens, it could take some time to work through.

You could have a buyer that is as interested in buying your property as you are in selling it. It could be the mortgage company or bank that causes you to lose the contract. You could have someone working on the financing that does not know what they are doing, so they require more information than is necessary to close a loan or is just wishy-washy about getting things finished. All of these things could drag a contract out beyond the closing date. The delays can also cause problems ending in a lost contract. If things drag on too long the buyers guaranteed interest rate could expire. This can result in further delays either for making adjustments or in a change in financial institutions. Circumstances in an individual's credit rating could change things and cause a delay.

Each delay or lost contract can increase your stress level. It can also scare away potential buyers and cause other complications. You will want to keep your wits and emotions in check. I would suggest that you not make any decisions based on expectations of your closing. You should continue your business as usual.

Each lost contract makes it more difficult to market your property. Your agent will be asked to explain what happened to the prior contract. If there are problems with the house it will make it more difficult to sell. Other agents understand the loss of a job or financing before they will forgive any problems with the home.

Beware of foundation issues. For those of us that live on a

clay soil, it is much easier to understand the issues that can arise season to season. As a matter of fact, this type of soil will have a lot to do with any problems the foundation can experience. The soil will expand and contract with the weather conditions. A wetter season will leave the ground more swollen and a drier season will cause the soil to shrink. If the soil is a rich one, there could be fewer disturbances whereas a clay soil will have a greater give and take. Minor seasonal changes will not necessarily require foundation repairs. The amount of watering you do can also affect the soil around your home. It does not require a rain to make changes in the soil moisture.

Before foundation repairs can be made, be sure to find out as much as you can. Besides multiple quotes for fixing a foundation, you will want to make sure that you understand the type of repairs that are needed. There are a number of techniques for fixing a foundation and each one comes with a different cost. The type soil you have will affect the type repair you will need. If you are not aware of the issues that will crop up from improper repairs, it can cost you in time, money and emotional upheaval.

The company you choose for your repairs is of the greatest importance. Remember that their warranty is only as good as the issuer. A lot of companies doing foundation repair come and go. Look for someone that has been around for a while and that has a good reputation. Also be sure the repair and warranty comes with an engineer's report. This report could be four or five hundred dollars but it is worth it in the long run. Because you can find out a good deal on the internet today, it is much easier to research the companies you consider.

CHAPTER THIRTEEN

The List

We have discussed a lot of things that can happen when you Buy, Rent or Sell, but there is more to it. Owning a house has so many responsibilities and there are issues that can rise from every one of them. There is no doubt that this book does not cover everything but it covers a lot. Here's a list of things you want to know that can happen.

Here are things we may or may not have covered when Buying and/or Selling!
- Finding an agent
- Marketing
- Showing
- Contracts
- Extensions
- Interest Rates
- Asking Price
- Negotiations
- Appraisals
- Engineers
- Inspectors
- Foundations
- Foundation companies
- Permits
- Improvements
- Closing Costs
- Loan Approvals
- Mortgage Companies
- Buyers
- Unknown liens

- Getting your name right

Things we may or may not have covered about Renting.
- Background checks
- Credit checks
- Financial obligations
- Lying renters
- Entitled renters
- Great expectations
- Is this a section 8?
- They broke it, who fixes it?
- Get it in writing
- Landlord vs. friend
- Get a receipt
- You still are obligated to the lease
- Security deposit vs. rent
- Security deposit breakdown
- Inspect going in
- Inspect going out
- Taking pictures
- The hidden boarder
- Pets or no pets?
- Pet type and deposits
- Citations and who is responsible
- Renters reporting you to agencies, newspapers or authorities.

Ways something can go wrong with a house
- Air Conditioner
  - has to be replaced
  - needs Freon
  - has other problems

- drain not connected to outside
- Heating Unit
  - goes out
  - put on breaker with not enough voltage
- Water heater
  - goes out
  - release valve not drained properly
  - not vented properly
- Gas leak
  - at water heater valve
- at stove valve
  - at fire place valve
  - somewhere
  - Gas line breaks
- Termites
- Mice
- Snakes & other critters
- Broken rafters
- Wiring
  - chewed
  - improperly done
  - outdated
  - Where's the light switch?
  -
- Plugs need replacing
- GFCI plugs in kitchen & bathroom
- Foundation issues
  - Ground swell in foundation
  - Shifting or dropped foundation
  - Improper foundation
  - Doors catawampus
  - Doors sticking
  - Cracks in walls begin to separate

- Ceiling cracks
- Plumbing Issues
  - Slab leak
  - Toilet leak
  - Pipes under sink leak
  - Ice maker line disconnected
  - Ice maker line leaks
  - Pipes stopped up
  - Ceiling leaks
  - Plumbing fixtures wear out
  - Sewer leakage
  - Sewer stoppage
  - Roots in sewer
  - Improper cleanout access
  -
- Chimney leaks
-
- Hail damage
- Roof damage due to falling limbs
- Fire place
  - opening improper size
  - cement cap to be replaced
  - flashing around roof replaced
  - damper not working
  - clean out leaking
  - pulling away from the wall
- Water leak around foundation
- Tile cracked
- Holes in walls
- Ceiling fan breaks
- Missing light bulbs
- Missing or broken switch plates
- Missing or broken plug covers

- Popcorn ceilings or other dated décor techniques
- Missing dry wall
- Stove goes out
- Refrigerator goes out
- Ice maker goes out
- Appliance lights go out
- Dishwasher
  - will not dry dishes
  - shorts out
  - breaks
- Washing machine
  - handle comes off
  - breaks
- Clothes Dryer
  - breaks
  - does not vent to outside
- Porch light goes out
- Gutters clog
- Hedges overgrow
- Water stands in yard
- Trees begin to die
- Tub/shower tile has to be re-grouted or replaced
- Time passes and styles change
- Counter tops cracked
- Toilet seats break
- Gutters wear out
- Limbs scrap the roof
- Sidewalk/driveway bumps
- City works on the street in front of your house
- Shower doors break
- Door knob falls off
- Garage door spring breaks
- Garage door opener fails
- Water sprinkler

- head breaks
- system line breaks or is cut
➢ Fence gets old
➢ Dog chews fence
➢ Shed gets flooded
➢ Lawn mower breaks
➢ Weed eater breaks
➢ Run out of closet space
➢ Floor gets scratched or gouged
➢ Porcelain chips in sink or tub
➢ Shower seat breaks
➢ Mirror cracks
➢ Garbage disposal wear out
➢ Garbage compactor breaks
➢ Vents need cleaning or replacing
➢ Dryer
➢ Door stopper missing
➢ Towel rack miscalculations
➢ Weather stripping
➢ The threshold leaks air
➢ Painting
- wall goes to the next room
- want to add or change color
- needs updating
➢ Double pane or single pane windows
➢ I thought the house was finished
➢ Why was the house constructed that way –ugly touches/major construction issues

WOW! What a list. It's enough to make you run away. But remember that if you are not buying, you are going to be that renter. The costs you have are due to how all renters respond. An owner needs to protect their property and the more costs they have in doing that, the more cost are passed on to renters. If you are renting, please respect the property and treat it like your own home.

The upside is that not all of these things are going to go wrong with your property. And, the things that do go wrong are probably not going to happen at once. Also, the more you know, the better prepared you are for anything that does happen. With the purchase of property, you earn equity which can be accessed when you sell. The more "extra" principle you pay each month, the greater your equity in your property.

Now that you have all this information, please do not let it discourage you from moving forward. These lists of what can go wrong are just for information. Owning a home is a great blessing. Investing, when done right, can be beneficial and rewarding.

PUBLICATIONS BY THE AUTHOR

We hope you will enjoy reading further publications by Pamela Flynt Knight. Hopefully you will find a touch of humor in _Rude Awakening or Not in the Budget._ This true story outlines the struggles the author encountered in eight years of an investment property. It began many of the experiences that are the foundation for _100+ Things That Can Go Wrong._ We hope it will prove helpful in your real estate endeavors.

All of Pamela Flynt Knight's books can be found at www.mgf-ventures.com. She has authored a book of poetry called _Sufficient Grace_; a spiritual book called _Living In The Fire_ and a history book co-authored with Richard G. Waller called _Legendary Locals of Grand Prairie_. Living in the Fire is currently being revised and a new additional should be released in 2018.

And, watch for upcoming publications; _Why Are You Here?_ to be released late in 2017 to celebrate the 25 years of the Pregnancy Resource Center of Grand Prairie (all proceeds go to help the PRC.); and _Standing on the Promises_, another spiritual book, is to be released sometime in 2018.

www.ingramcontent.com/pod-product-compliance
Lightning Source LLC
Chambersburg PA
CBHW071806170526
45167CB00003B/1195